Wine, Wipes & Just Happene

The Funny Gift Book Every New Mum Actually Needs

By **Sleepless Press**

Copyright Page

Wine, Wipes & What Just Happened?
© 2025 Sleepless Press

This book is intended for entertainment purposes only. While it contains light-hearted tips, it is not a substitute for professional parenting advice (or for sleep).

First Edition, 2025

Published by Sleepless Press

Printed in the United Kingdom / United States via Kindle Direct Publishing

Dedication

For every new mum who's ever reheated the same cup of tea three times,
worn yoghurt as an accessory,
or wondered if they're the only one winging it.

You're not.
This book is for you.

(And also for wine. And chocolate. Always chocolate.)

Table of Contents

Motherhood: where your phone is full, your fridge is empty, and your heart is somehow both.

Introduction

Motherhood: the only job where the boss screams, never sleeps, and pays you in cuddles.

Welcome to your new reality — where your hot tea is always cold, your laundry multiplies faster than rabbits, and your Google search history reads like a medical drama.

This book won't tell you how to swaddle like a pro, puree organic veg at 6 a.m., or sleep-train without muttering expletives under your breath. There are plenty of manuals, experts, and glossy Instagram posts for that.

This is not that.

This is the survival guide you actually need — the one that admits biscuits count as breakfast, that sometimes the buggy feels like an Olympic sport, and that yes, you absolutely will cry at a Christmas advert while clutching a box of tissues.

It's not here to give you instructions. It's here to give you a laugh.

Inside these pages, you'll find:

- **The Daily Grind** — midnight Googling, nap traps, and the eternal question: "Why is there glitter in my hair?"

- **The Survival Hacks** — coffee, chocolate, and hiding in the bathroom (the holy trinity).

- **The Relatable Truths** — the photos, the meltdowns, the stories every mum secretly shares.

- **The Magic Bits** — the first laugh, the unexpected cuddles, the moments that make you think, "Okay, maybe I *can* do this."

It's part travel guide, part diary, part therapy session in book form.

Because here's the thing: you're not supposed to have it all together. Nobody does. Every mum — even the ones with matching outfits and spotless kitchens on Instagram — has had a WHAT JUST HAPPENED moment (or seventeen) today.

So if all you've managed this morning is to get dressed (kind of) and keep a small human alive, congratulations. You're winning.

So grab this book. Stash it in the nappy bag. Shove it between the wipes and the emergency chocolate. Flip through whenever you need reminding that you're not alone, you're doing brilliantly, and yes — it really is this ridiculous.

A Note to Gift-Givers

If you're holding this book but not holding a baby, chances are you're here for one reason: you're about to make a new mum laugh (and probably cry a little too).

Good choice.

New mums don't need another muslin, a fifteenth cuddly toy, or yet another well-meaning lecture about "sleeping when the baby sleeps." What they *do* need is a reminder that they're not alone, that it's okay to find the chaos hilarious, and that biscuits in the bathroom count as self-care.

So if you're giving this book, know this: you're basically handing over the gift of sanity. You are a hero. There should be a medal. (But since there isn't, go ahead and eat a celebratory Jaffa Cake on the way home.)

Part 1: The Essentials

🍷 Wine

Once upon a time, wine meant Friday nights, candlelight, and actual conversation.
Now? Wine means:

- Half a glass poured at 8 p.m., forgotten until 10:30 p.m.

- A lukewarm sip between sterilising bottles.

- Falling asleep with your face in the sofa cushion before you finish it.

Mum Hack: It doesn't matter if it's red, white, or rosé. If it's wet and vaguely alcoholic, it's medicinal.

MUM'S
SURVIVAL
GLASS

📦 Wipes

They're not just wipes. They're civilisation's most powerful invention. One packet, infinite uses:

- Cleaning the baby.

- Cleaning the floor.

- Cleaning the car seat.

- Cleaning your mascara when you've cried at yet another TV advert.

- Emergency "shower."

Traveller Warning: If you leave the house without wipes, fate *will* punish you.

Baby Wipes™

Tagline: The Swiss Army Knife of Parenthood.
Uses: Cleaning hands, faces, bums, the sofa, and the car dashboard.
Side Effects: A packet in every pocket, bag, and glove compartment.

😱 WHAT JUST HAPPENED Moments

Parenting is full of tiny miracles. And then there are the other moments — the ones that make you stop and ask: *what fresh chaos is this?*

- When the baby sneezes directly into your eyeball.

- When you find raisins in the bed (and you don't even own raisins).

- When the nappy situation looks like an abstract art installation.

- When silence lasts too long, and you know you're doomed.

Mum Hack: Laugh. Or cry. Or both. You're doing it right.

Biscuit Break 🍪

Self-care, one digestive at a time.

Part 2: The Daily Grind

🫖 Cold Tea (and Other Broken Dreams)

You make it. You pour it. You put it down. And there it sits, stone cold, abandoned, like a sad little puddle of hope. By the time you actually drink it, it tastes like regret.

Mum Hack: Accept it. Rebrand it. Call it *iced tea* and pretend you're chic.

Cold Tea

(and Other Broken Dreams)

 Laundry Mountain

You once dreamed of climbing Kilimanjaro. Now, you're scaling Mount Laundry. It regenerates daily, like some sort of fabric-based Hydra. Each time you slay one load, three more appear.

Climbers report:

- Baby vests multiplying in the dark.

- Tiny socks vanishing into another dimension.

- Damp muslins that never, ever dry.

Traveller Warning: Sherpas (also known as partners) may mysteriously disappear when laundry duty is mentioned.

🎭 Car Seat Wrestling

Forget yoga. Forget CrossFit. The true sport of parenthood is wrestling a wriggling octopus disguised as a baby into a car seat.

Round 1: Baby stiffens into plank mode.
Round 2: Screaming commences.
Round 3: You break into a sweat, muttering "just let me clip the buckle!"

Mum Hack: Bribery doesn't work yet. Deep breathing *might*. Earplugs *will*.

🍴 The 3 p.m. Snack Crisis

It's always 3 p.m. Someone is always hungry. And somehow, it's always the one snack you *don't* have.

You could have a fridge full of food, a cupboard stocked with treats, and a bag rattling with emergency breadsticks — and still, disaster will strike.

The raisins? Wrong brand.
The biscuits? Broken.
The banana? Too bendy.
The apple? *"Yucky."*

Apparently, snacks must meet exacting toddler standards that shift hourly and are often impossible to predict. (Yesterday, crackers were life. Today, crackers are poison.)

So you offer alternatives. One by one. And one by one, they are rejected with all the drama of a Shakespearean tragedy. Meanwhile, the clock ticks toward dinner and you find yourself wondering whether you should just serve spaghetti hoops at 3:15 p.m. and call it a night.

Traveller's Warning: the 3 p.m. Snack Crisis is not a one-off. It's a daily feature of the itinerary. Some days it passes quickly; other days it escalates into a full-scale meltdown in aisle four of Tesco while you clutch multipacks of Jaffa Cakes and wonder where it all went wrong.

Pro Tip: Always keep a stash for yourself. Hide biscuits in the bathroom. Keep chocolate in the airing cupboard. No one ever needs to know. (This is known in the trade as *parent self-care*.)

And remember: broken biscuits still taste the same. At least for you.

THE 3 P.M. SNACK CRISIS

Hide a stash of **biscuits for yourself.**
Eat them in the bathroom if necessary.
(This is known as parent self-care.)

Broken biscuits still taste the same.

🛒 Supermarket Safari

The wildest jungle on earth isn't in the Amazon. It *is* Amazon. Or Tesco. Or Aldi. Wherever you dare to venture, you'll face:

- Public meltdowns.

- Judgy stares.

- A till that breaks down the moment you're finally next in line.

Traveller Warning: Never shop hungry. You'll come home with six multipacks of Jaffa Cakes and no nappies.

📱 Midnight Googling

The soundtrack of The Daily Grind: frantic 2 a.m. Googling.

- "Is 4 sneezes in a row normal?"

- "Can a baby survive solely on air and toast crusts?"

- "Why is there glitter in my hair?"

Mum Hack: Step away from Dr. Google. The answer is always: "it's normal." (Unless it's *really not* — in which case, call someone qualified.)

This Page Reserved for Cold Tea Stains

(If yours doesn't land here eventually,

you're not reading it right.)

Part 3: The Nights

🌙 Midnight Google Searches

It starts with one sneeze. One innocent sneeze. Next thing you know, it's 2:37 a.m. and you've gone down a digital rabbit hole.

- "Can babies dream about milk?"

- "What does green poo mean?"

- "How long can a human survive on no sleep?"
  Spoiler: Don't Google it. You won't like the answers.

Mum Hack: Switch the phone off. Or at least stop before you reach page 7 of Mumsnet.

Top 5 Things You'll Definitely Google at 2 a.m.

1. Is my baby broken or just noisy?
2. How long can humans survive without REM sleep?
3. Why does my baby hiccup like a tiny tractor?
4. Can caffeine be delivered via IV?
5. What day is it?

🎤 The 2 a.m. Crying Concert

Forget Glastonbury. The hottest ticket in town is the Baby Crying Concert, playing nightly in your bedroom. One act, one stage, no encore, no refunds. Audience participation required.

Traveller Warning: May continue for the rest of the night. Earplugs optional. Sanity questionable.

🔖 The Bedtime Riddle

How many parents does it take to put one baby to bed?
Answer: Infinite. One to bounce, one to rock, one to Google
"bedtime routine," and eventually all of them to collapse in
despair.

Mum Hack: The trick is... oh wait. There isn't one.

⛑ The 45-Minute Nap Trap

You finally get them down. You tiptoe out. You make tea, sit down, exhale—
And then, *WAAAAAAAH*.
The mythical "long nap" is a fairy tale passed down by smug parents.

Pro Tip: Never, ever say out loud, "They're sleeping well tonight." You'll jinx it.

The 45-Minute Nap Trap

WAAAAAAH!

SLEEPLESS PRESS

Red Wine Rings Go Here

(Perfectly acceptable bookmark system.)

🌀 Night-Time Hallucinations

At some point, the exhaustion gets so real you'll swear the laundry pile moved, the cat just spoke, or your partner asked you to "pass the baby" when they weren't even in the room.

Mum Hack: Embrace it. Consider it free entertainment.

Night-Time Hallucinations

This page left intentionally blank for emergency naps.

Part 4: The Survival Hacks

🍫 The Emergency Chocolate Stash

Rule one of motherhood: always know where your chocolate is.
Cupboard? Too obvious.
Freezer? Smart.
Behind the stack of muslins in the airing cupboard? Genius.
Because when the day has been long and the night looks longer, only chocolate understands.

Mum Hack: Buy the multipack "for the kids." Eat them yourself.

THE EMERGENCY
CHOCOLATE STASH

👜 Snacks in Every Pocket

You'll find yourself carrying snacks like a squirrel hoards nuts. One in the coat pocket. One in the handbag. Three in the car. A rogue breadstick in the buggy.

Traveller Warning: Be prepared to discover a six-month-old rice cake when you least expect it. (And yes, it will still look edible. Don't.)

Top 5 Places You'll Find Raisins

1. Cot
2. Car seat
3. Your bra
4. Handbag lining
5. Mystery location still undiscovered

☕ Coffee = Personality Replacement

Coffee doesn't just wake you up. Coffee is you now. Without it, you're a husk. With it, you're a goddess capable of holding entire conversations that vaguely make sense.

Mum Hack: Invest in the biggest mug you can find. Or go pro and upgrade to a travel flask.

Mum Fuel Coffee™

Tasting Notes: *Burnt, lukewarm, occasionally reheated three times.*
Pairs With: *Biscuits in the bathroom.*

🧦 The Spare Top Rule

One spare top for the baby is rookie level.
One spare top for you? Expert.
Because sooner or later, you *will* end up wearing a questionable liquid. And you will *not* want to smell of it in public.

Pro Tip: Black hides a multitude of stains. Sequins, less so.

Packing Checklist (Spoof Version)

- ☑ 4 nappies
- ☑ 2 wipes packets
- ☑ 1 muslin
- ☑ 1 spare top (for baby)
- ☑ 1 spare top (for me)
- ☑ 37 biscuits

📺 Netflix and (Definitely No) Chill

Forget box sets for relaxation. Now it's background noise while you fold laundry at midnight. But still—bless Netflix. Without it, the small hours would be very, very lonely.

Mum Hack: Subtitle everything. You'll never hear the dialogue over the crying anyway.

Part 5: The Relatable Truths

😭 Crying at Adverts

Forget hormones. Parenthood turns you into a walking tear machine.

- Puppies in slow motion? Tears.

- A Christmas advert with a lonely snowman? Sobs.

- Anything with a baby? Total emotional collapse.

Mum Hack: Stock tissues. And maybe avoid *The Repair Shop* until you're emotionally stable (so... 2047).

CHRISTMAS ADVERT

📷 4,532 Baby Photos

You will take more photos of your baby in the first six months than you took of yourself in the last six years. 99% of them will look identical. But delete one? Never.

Traveller Warning: Phone storage will run out before your sleep does.

🍼 Instagram vs Reality

On Instagram: a serene mum in cashmere, sipping a latte, baby sleeping peacefully.
In reality: You, in yoghurt-stained pyjamas, cold tea in hand, baby wide awake and sticky.

Pro Tip: Post the latte pic anyway. Nobody needs to know.

Top 5 Mum Accessories

1. Under-eye bags
2. Cold tea mug
3. Messy bun (mandatory)
4. Giant tote bag
5. The "is it bedtime yet?" face

❤️ The First Laugh

Amidst the chaos, something magical happens. The first laugh. It's pure, perfect, and worth every sleepless night, every cold tea, every WHAT JUST HAPPENED moment.

Mum Hack: Record it. Replay it. Remember: this is why you keep going.

THE FIRST LAUGH

The first laugh is worth every sleepless night.

🧟 Winging It

The biggest truth of all: nobody has a clue what they're doing. Not the mums at baby yoga. Not the bloggers. Not even your mum. We're all improvising, every single day.

Insider Tip: You don't need a plan. You just need coffee, wipes, and a sense of humour.

Emergency Mum Bingo

- ✅ Cold tea
- ✅ Crying in Tesco car park
- ✅ Chocolate for breakfast
- ✅ Baby sick in hair
- ✅ Texted partner "WHERE ARE YOU?!" in all caps

Final Word

Motherhood is wild.

It's sticky, noisy, exhausting, and completely unpredictable. It's sleepless nights, cold tea, and conversations with Google at 3 a.m. It's a to-do list that never ends, laundry piles that multiply overnight, and a fridge that's somehow always out of milk.

But it's also something else.
It's belly laughs that come out of nowhere.
It's tiny hands reaching for yours.
It's cuddles that make your heart burst and melt away a whole day's worth of stress in a single moment.
It's the magic of the first laugh, the wobble of first steps, and the knowledge that—despite the madness—you are someone's whole world.

So if you take nothing else from this book, let it be this:

You are not doing it wrong.
It *is* this hard.
And you are doing brilliantly.

There are no gold medals for perfectly folded laundry, no prizes for keeping your baby in colour-coordinated outfits. There's only the daily marathon of showing up, loving hard, and winging it as best you can. And that's more than enough.

When in doubt:

- Reach for coffee. ☕

- Break into the emergency chocolate. 🍫

- Hide in the bathroom with biscuits if you must. 🍪

- Laugh at the madness whenever you can. 😂

Because one day, these WHAT JUST HAPPENED moments will become the stories you tell with a grin. They'll be the "Remember when…?" memories you share with friends, the ones that bond you to every other mum who's been in the trenches too.

And when you look back, you'll see what you couldn't always see in the middle of the chaos: you were stronger, funnier, braver, and more brilliant than you gave yourself credit for.

So here's to you, Mum.
To your cold tea, your hidden chocolate stash, your late-night Googling, and your endless love.

You've got this.
You've always had this.

Now go on—reheat that tea (again). You've earned it.

Top 5 Signs You're Doing Brilliantly

1. Baby is alive ✓
2. You are alive ✓
3. Everyone has eaten something (biscuits count)
4. Someone laughed today ✓
5. You found time to read this book ✓

Close the book. Open the wine.

SLEEPLESS
PRESS

Printed in Dunstable, United Kingdom